The Salt Before It Shakes

poems

Yvonne Stephens

HIDDEN TIMBER BOOKS
MEANINGFUL BOOKS AND STORIES

Milwaukee, Wisconsin

"Peach Petals Like the Cheeks of That Girl" first appeared in the 44th edition of *Patterns* (2002), a publication of St. Clair County Community College.

"Taking in the Sun" was selected to be part of the multi-media project, "Rooting Deep Branching Out," a partnership of the Jordan River Arts Council and the Institute for Sustainable Living, Art and Natural Design (2009).

"Porcupine" first appeared online in the LAND (Liberal Arts Network for Development) *Creative Writing Journal* (2011), and was awarded First Place in the LAND Poetry Competition.

"Jeff Daniels and Me at the Partial Hospitalization Program" first appeared in the *Dunes Review* (Fall/Winter 2015), and was nominated for the Pushcart Prize.

Hidden Timber Books LLC
5464 N Port Washington Rd #C224
Milwaukee, WI 53217
www.hiddentimberbooks.com

The Salt Before It Shakes / Yvonne Stephens — 1st ed.
ISBN 978-0-9906530-5-9

For Jason

Acknowledgements

This chapbook would not be possible without the generosity, guidance, support and vision of Lisa Rivero and Hidden Timber Books. Thank you for making my dream come true, this chapbook debut. For you, I am forever grateful.

I am indebted to Cristina Norcross for her sharp skills as editor, Holly Wren Spaulding for being my poetry-midwife, mentor, instructor and friend, and the excellent literary citizenship of Patricia Ann McNair, the Interlochen Writers Retreat, and Michigan Writers.

The large community of family, friends, poets and writers who helped me be who I am so I could write these poems also includes, but is not limited to: Laura Foster, Jim Frank, Diane Wakoski, Jenny Robertson, Katey Schultz, Tanya Muzumdar, Christi Craig, Peter and Mary LeTourneau, John and Pat Stephens, Dr. Lawrence Probes, and, of course, Jason, Jacob and Tilia.

To all the rest of my family and friends who live and no longer live in Antrim County, in Michigan, Wisconsin, Texas and beyond, I give thanks.

Contents

EVEN NOW
~ *Xalapa, Veracruz, Mexico*

Burying a horse takes time
two men
some Xalapan sun.

Sun to bake the soil
the new bones,
all the bones it ever had —

Are the bones still tucked
in the folds of that field?
Soil has an appetite —
can it end?

Yvonne Stephens

AS A DIGNITY
~ for M. Toth

I remember talking to my grandfather after he passed,
sensing he was still in his body,
thanking him for the tractor rides, his garden, his orchard —
Hungarian peppers, apple picking, cherries.

The blood dripping from his nose,
the nurse wiping it away.
Our custom to drain it,
as a dignity. The make-up.
"He looks just like him."
"He looks peaceful."

We tucked his ripe tomatoes in with him,
the first of the season —
his unfinished bottle of Jim Beam,
drawings from great-grandchildren.

His urn sits on the mantle he built
under the ship he painted and framed.
My grandmother lives in their house,
with his ship, their mantel, 62 years of marriage,
now some fresh paint, carpet, linens.
Doublemint gum is in the cupboard.

Yvonne Stephens

Below the mirror in the basement, his shaving kit.
So as to be quiet, a quiet shave early in the morning,
so as not to disturb my grandmother while she slept.
He shaved in preparation for his daily walk,
for church, and I'd guess,
for his outpatient surgery that day.

ELEVEN MOPS
~ *after Wallace Stevens*

Three things that flop like a mop: a lump of spaghetti, a wet t-shirt, bread dough.

Some witches fly on brooms. It takes a certain witch to whistle by on a wet mop.

Before you mop, squeeze out some water — too much leaves a dull film.

You are five and riding a mop-stick-horse — your shadow gallops with you.

The words mom and pop both differ by one letter — from mop.

Crossing a mop to and fro can lead to a clean floor and should lead to a Cajun waltz.

When Mrs. Boyd lost her husband, we went to her house to sweep, dust, and mop.

As I work a mop around my feet, there it is: a microphone, the urge to sing.

To some, a bottle of tequila and a mop stick means in about an hour, it's limbo time.

I think of this green handled mop as a daisy — do you love me or do you love my mop?

A mop dipped in kerosene and this lit match leap like a blackbird taking flight.

Yvonne Stephens

PORCUPINE
~ after Fleda Brown

Say porcupine, pickle, quill:
all second cousins once removed,
the way you and I might be cousins,
how we love bacon and crossword puzzles,
and crumple newspaper to light the woodstove.
Feel the way they pick the tongue
like a French kiss with braces,
but turn soft, like a fish bone composts
into soil, and ripens into tomato.
A porcupine snaps a kosher dill,
stabs a sheet of paper with a quill
and pencils the message, "If I could speak,
my voice would sound like caterpillar frass
falling through the canopy." This may be
a good place to stop. It's true,
a porcupine would have lovely
handwriting, a perfect calligraphy.
He writes to remind us that, once,
there was no other way. Since we can't
lick a stamp, let's cheer for the porcupine
who chews the bark of a healthy tree,

shifts it from the chainsaw, to the insects
and birds. Let's give them the salt they crave
and die for on the roads. Here I am hunched
over its carcass collecting quills. Here I am
hunched over my dog, pulling quills from her face
with pliers. Porcupines turn their backs
toward their foes, which is how I enter this cold lake,
and become wrapped in a pelt, soft and sharp.

GIVE ME A BUSHEL OF TOMATOES

and I'll can them.
Drop into a rhythm
of blanch, peel, core, slice.

This year I will can enough to feed us,
the neighbors, and their grandkids —
because I can.

I can all my free time away.
I freeze, dry, cellar, ferment, pickle —
put food by to call on winter.

When I am done and I can
look from applesauce
all the way back to pickled leeks,
the growing season on shelves,
in glass, vacuum-sealed —

I'll be ready to open those leeks in November
and remember my third month on fertility drugs,
then fourth, fifth.

We'll recall my laparoscopic surgery
over strawberry freezer jam on toast in February.
One, two, three incisions, scars the size of buttonholes.

Apricots in light syrup —
our first pregnancy
after 2½ years of trying.

Bread and butter pickles,
dilly beans, peaches, and tomatoes —
the month of our miscarriage.

I can make fruit last.
I can make spring, summer, and fall last
in Ball jars and Ziploc freezer bags.

This winter, I will haul out summer
from the chest freezer
tart cherries to suck on, to make pie.

You and I are omnivorous —
even bitter fruit, somehow,
sustains us.

ASH

Ash logs burn in the woodstove
the emerald borer feasts in the dark

Color where there seems to be no color
ash where there seems to be no ash

Spin like a tire on ash on ice
wish for the grip and turn

Yvonne Stephens

THE FOUR OF US

Loyal lips, tongues, fingers, feet.
Hope is you in your suit,
blue blue blue, indigo blue.
Loyal, the dog in the corner
covered in song —

Freedom is mouth open to sky,
hope is your billowy dress,
it becomes fish.
Freedom, gills in the water
a kind of song —

Fear is our quiet eyes.
Hope is the movement
to the streets.
Until then, it's the four of us —
the salt before it shakes.

Yvonne Stephens

RECREATION CENTER

Dance class, I was a cabbage patch,
I got yelled at for licking the bar.
It was salty.

5th Grade Basketball games —
Twizzlers and Better Mades
rumble of feet on the bleachers.

One time, my brother was late
he offered apology, I remember apology
I didn't want apology.

The salty bar, the salty chips
red licorice —
the hum of the lights gone quiet.

Yvonne Stephens

RE-CREATION

At this past mass shooting
I heard there were busloads of survivors
brought to their families
brought to a community building —

The families waited for hours in the gym,
busloads brought to them.
Then no more buses.
Then police.
Then I'm sorry, I'm sorry, I'm sorry.

Yvonne Stephens

I THINK OF COYOTES

I didn't feel like walking, but we went.
October, cold, spitting rain.
Our dog happy to be out.

I kept seeing the deer's mangled body
two broken legs. You said,
think of the coyotes instead.

The field, thick with mist and moonlight,
round hay bales, shadows.
Hunters and scavengers at work.

And, dear, I do think of coyotes —
how they shift
how they are clever.

Yvonne Stephens

BLOODLETTING

Mine slid out like an amoeba —
stretched into a rectangle,
became recognizable
as the state of Montana.

I've always wanted to visit
its grasshopper glacier,
sapphires, big sky.
So, I step in its puddle,

and end up in Decorah, Iowa —
hometown of an old friend.
I sent a letter with no reply.
It's been years.

"Hug me, I'm bloodletting?"
"Hug me, I donated?"
Nope, just a draw.
Cool swipe, inner elbow prick.

My arm, a ukulele unplugged,
the phlebotomist plucks its string.
Pesky-hide-and-seek-playing vein
she pulls the needle out, tries again.

I push away thoughts of embolisms
and sepsis, think instead:
"What is it this time
they'll call and recommend?"

The sticker I wear home
doesn't ask for anything.
Just a Band-Aid over a cotton ball,
it looks like a leech.

Later, when I peel it off,
I find the rust-colored "o" of a mouth
then I give it a kiss
and lay its limp body down.

DELIVER THIS BODY

I want to be lacerated
by an alligator's vise grip —
stone ground to bits
by its gastroliths.

Or better yet, poisoned.
I want Amanita fever to
deliver my kidney and liver
to ocean, brine.

I want a tree limb,
to find my curious head —
hammer it into the loamy ground
on which it stands.

Leave me here to become
mother of maggots
that feed birds
that feed bullfrogs.

Or, consumed by wildfire.
Not even two bones left to bang together.
As ash, I will travel the wind
like dust, like pollen, like seed.

Yvonne Stephens

CROOKED RIB

As a kid I heard that Brooke Shields,
or maybe Cher,
had a few lower ribs removed —
cosmetic reasons.

I had a Brooke Shields Barbie Doll
and a Barbie RV. My brother
pushed them down the stairs,
Brooke's head broke off.
She was never the same.

Cher wanted to turn back time —
I just wanted to grow boobs.
Skinny, all that
stuck out was my rib.

I would not recommend
smoking it. Maybe it is a
harp or an archer's bow.
Could be lucky
like a horseshoe.

Yvonne Stephens

Postpartum, that rib is
covered up, padded.
My aunt and uncle
each have crooked ribs, too.

This rib, you might not want it.
Didn't I mention it's crooked?

I sleep on my left side,
and this rib tucks in, just right.
Crooked rib of mine.

TO BUILD A SAUNA

and uphold a Finnish tradition
because I'm ¼ Finn
and you,
you love saunas.

You have wanted a sauna for some time.
I'll build it by hand —
make it round or oval.

Someone once told me
the absence of corners
gives the sauna
a womb-like feel.

Since I can't give birth
we could get born
out of this small room I built
to sit in with you.

Taking a sauna
can be good for your health.
It can be good to sit and sweat
then rinse it all away.
It can purify.

So, my love
while my hands are still able
I'd like to build a sauna for you.

PREGNANCY AFTER INFERTILITY
AFTER MISCARRIAGE

Stand among seven
lions' corpses, scorched

The one to the left stands up
shakes off black char

Grows a mane and coat
licks its forepaw

Through squinted eyes, asks
"What color are you
going to paint the nursery?"

Yvonne Stephens

TOMATO HORNWORM, A STUDY

In July, I couldn't keep you
off my tomato plants —
I put an end to your softness
with my shoe.

A drought year, a cold one, too —
tomatoes grew in tight curls
like your body.
They didn't have your eyes, though.

What is that horn for?
I'd like to see you use it.
I hear you chew.
I see what you leave behind.

Too soft to pluck,
a friend cuts you off with scissors —
there's an idea.

September, instead of tomatoes,
I seek you, caterpillar to cocoon.
Did my son scare you off?
The way he'd toddle over, bite
the green fruit?

Or was it the way I looked at you
with my lonely eyes?
It wouldn't be the first time.

JEFF DANIELS AND ME AT THE
PARTIAL HOSPITALIZATION PROGRAM

He sat across from me and sounded like Jeff Daniels.
I thought I was auditioning.
"Escanaba in da Moonlight," again?
We tried Finn, *sauna, Hauskaa Joulua.*

I thought I was auditioning.
I had to explain it was "Merry Christmas."
We tried Finn, *sauna, Hauskaa Joulua.*
Maybe I did my roots no good.

I had to explain it was "Merry Christmas."
Jeff Daniels stood across from me, a gallon Ziploc full of meds.
Maybe I did my roots no good.
I overheard his dog died the night before.

Jeff Daniels stood across from me, a gallon Ziploc full of meds.
I thought he was my estranged friend, Tom Wyse.
I overheard his dog died the night before.
I cried and said he reminded me of someone.

I thought he was my estranged friend, Tom Wyse.
He said he hoped it was good.
I cried and said he reminded me of someone.
At the end of the day, he said, "Be careful out there."

He said he hoped it was good.
And I swear he was Tom Wyse.
At the end of the day, he said, "Be careful out there."
I exited the building and followed a trail of apples.

And I swear he was Tom Wyse.
He sat across from me and sounded like Jeff Daniels.
I exited the building and followed a trail of apples.
I thought I was auditioning.

PEACH PETALS LIKE THE CHEEKS OF THAT GIRL

Dancing at the bus stop
long black curls flying
snowflakes trying
legs and head shaking
lavender coat on a snowy pile.

On the salted sidewalk
in the moments before
she may have crouched down
cupped her mittened-hands
laid her cheek down and listened.

Yvonne Stephens

WORKDAY'S END

I would watch my father
empty his pockets —
wallet then keys,
knife then change pouch.

The wash would take out
a nut, a dime,
sometimes Kleenex, torn to scrap.

I would help him take off his boots
that smelled like hot leather.
Sweat-metallic —

Cowboy-style, they required a bit of
pull and push and then pull
before they would give
to my small hands.

My father wore pocket T's
and 5-pocket blue jeans
hauled scrap metal with a HI-LO forklift.

Yvonne Stephens

Some days, he would lift me up
set me on his shoulders and say

Whoa, daughter, getting big on me!
I remember when you were just
knee high to a grasshopper!

I recall trying to imagine myself, then
when I could have fit in his pocket.

MY MOTHER

I think of the horses that will show up for her.
3, or 6 coming 2x2.
She'll be coming around the mountain when she goes.

Quilts in her wagon, blue hair blazing.
She will be the woman I've never known.
She will be the 20-something
having a drink at a bar in Germany.

She will be the woman my father showed up for
in a red alligator suit, dancing.
She'll be the Mary K. Toth turned LeTourneau.

The high-schooler who taught herself to sew.
The 9-month-old who potty trained herself.
Why my daughter has curls.

She'll be the child at her grandfather's house on the lake,
and the tornado that came.
She'll be the tornado that came.
She will be the tornado.
She'll be.

Yvonne Stephens

IMMINENT RAIN

post drought
dark clouds
rumble

branches, leaves
shake
vibration

down the cambium
yes, roots
soon, drink —

Yvonne Stephens

TAKING IN THE SUN

Cut in to the sun-lit-up top
of the river with my canoe oar.

Sliced out as big a piece as I could get,
slid it into the basket at my hip like a fish.

Took my chunk of sun home,
put it in a jar with some yeast.

The yeast fed
on the sweetness of the sun.

Fished out the glowing spheres
of carbonation with a spoon —

as many as I could get.
Lined them up

around the base of my neck
and wore the sun.

Yvonne Stephens

WHAT REMAINS

of this blue jay —
a pile of feathers,
downy, quills.

No blood.

Even in a slight breeze
feathers stir
shift, start.

Yvonne Stephens

SCROLLING MY NEWSFEED

I collect stones:
war, climate
death by bullet.

Later, I drive by Craven Pond,
thin with ice, thick with geese
each standing on one leg —

I pull over
finger the pond in my palm,
my fortune of stones.

What are geese called
when they gather?
How do they handle the cold?

Tell me, does the ice melt first?
The gaggle of geese disperse?
What exactly is the word for end?

About the Author

Yvonne Stephens lives with her husband and two children in Northwest Lower Michigan. She has worked as an assistant in the fields of mycology, forestry, and neurology research, volunteered for two years in the AmeriCorps, and most recently was an Artist Residency Coordinator for the Crosshatch Center for Art and Ecology. An award-winning poet, Yvonne was nominated for the Pushcart Prize in 2015, and her poems have appeared in the *Dunes Review*, the *LAND Creative Writing Journal*, and *Family Stories from the Attic*. Visit her blog at poetwith40eyes.com.

Made in the USA
Columbia, SC
28 January 2018